Written by Heather Camlot
Illustrated by Mike Deas

I CAN'T Do WHAT?

Strange Laws and Rules from Around the World

Red Deer Press

D1528834

Published in Canada by Red Deer Press, 209 Wicksteed Avenue, Unit 51, Toronto, ON M4G 0B1
Published in the United States by Red Deer Press, 311 Washington Street, Brighton, MA 02135

Red Deer Press acknowledges with thanks the Canada Council for the Arts and the Ontario Arts Council
for their support of our publishing program. We acknowledge the financial support of the
Government of Canada through the Canada Book Fund (CBF) for our publishing activities.

Library and Archives Canada Cataloguing in Publication
Title: I can't do what? : strange laws and rules from around the world / by Heather Camlot ;
illustrated by Mike Deas.
Names: Camlot, Heather, 1972 - author. | Deas, Mike, 1982- illustrator.
Description: Includes bibliographical references and index.
Identifiers: Canadiana 20210387505 | ISBN 9780889956186 (softcover)
Subjects: LCSH: Law—Cross-cultural studies—Juvenile literature. | LCSH: Social norms—Cross-cultural
studies—Juvenile literature. | LCSH: Law—Miscellanea—Juvenile literature. | LCSH: Social norms—
Miscellanea—Juvenile literature.
Classification: LCC K240 .C36 2022 | DDC j340—dc23

Publisher Cataloging-in-Publication Data (U.S.)
Names: Camlot, Heather, 1972 - author. | Deas, Mike, 1982-, illustrator.
Title: I Can't Do What : Strange Laws and Rules from Around the World / by Camlot, Heather, 1972-, author; illustrated
by Mike Deas. Description: Markham, Ontario : Red Deer Press, 2022.| Summary: "This book is a glance over many years
at rules and laws that have been created around the world. It is divided into four sections: people problems; sports zone;
entertainment interrupted; and kids' concerns. It features some of the funniest, scariest, most maddening and confusing
regulations leaving readers questioning just who makes the rules and how they might be changed." -- Provided by publisher.
Identifiers: ISBN 978-0-88995-618-6 (paperback)
Subjects: LCSH Law -- Humor — Juvenile Literature. | Law – Miscellanea – Juvenile literature. | BISAC: JUVENILE
NONFICTION / Law & Crime.
Classification: LCC K183.C365 |DDC 340.02 – dc23

The illustrations by Mike Deas were initially sketched on the computer using Wacom Cintiq, then printed,
traced onto thicker paper with brush and ink, and shaded using black watercolour.

Edited for the Press by Beverley Brenna
Text and cover design by Tanya Montini
Printed in Canada by AIIM– Avant Imaging & Integrated Media Inc.

www.reddeerpress.com

For Peter Carver, who understands my need
to dot the i's and cross the t's.
—H.C.

For Annie and Faye.
—M.D.

CONTENTS

WHAT CAN I DO?: While most entries in this book relate to one country at a time, it doesn't mean that rule or law isn't in others as well. It may even be in yours. Head to the library or go online and do some research to see what rules or laws prevail where you live. Make sure to look for at least three reputable online and/or print sources that say the same thing!

INTRODUCTION

Did you know that you can't keep a goldfish in a round goldfish bowl in Rome? That you can't take a selfie while running with the bulls in Pamplona? That you can't climb a tree in a Toronto city park? This book is a look at some of the more curious rules and laws that have been created around the world over many years. Both laws and rules are sets of instructions. Laws are created by the government to protect people's rights and freedoms and to maintain peace and order. They apply equally to a whole society, like no stealing or killing. Rules, on the other hand, are created by individuals or organizations and guide how to act and behave in particular situations, like no bullying in school or no using your football helmet as a weapon.

That football helmet rule is pretty strange, right? Sometimes we find things funny or weird because we don't understand them—especially when the rules or laws aren't from our own culture or country. Sometimes we just need to better understand why they were created to know whether they are as strange as they seem. When we learn more, we gain insight and can make clearer decisions about how we feel about something. Sometimes we know right away that

ONCE UPON A TIME: The Code of Hammurabi is one of the world's oldest collections of laws, dating back to the 18th century BCE. Hammurabi was a king who ruled over the Babylonian Empire (Iraq and Kuwait today). While the code is quite progressive in some cases, like innocent until proven guilty, it's also quite gruesome. For example: if you hit your father, you'd lose your hands. If you committed robbery, you'd be put to death. Yikes.

a rule or a law isn't good—that it reinforces wrong thinking about groups of people.

Understanding laws and rules means you understand how to act without getting into trouble. But it also means you can speak up when you see laws and rules being denied, broken, or disrespected— or when you disagree with them and believe they need to change.

Some of the rules and laws in *I Can't Do What?* may make you laugh. Some may make you mad. Some may make you scared. Others may make you think. Hopefully all will make you question why certain rules exist and why your country does or doesn't have similar ones.

> **This book is meant to inform and entertain, not to provide legal advice. Please consult a licensed legal professional for any issues with the law.**

SECTION 1

PEOPLE PROBLEMS

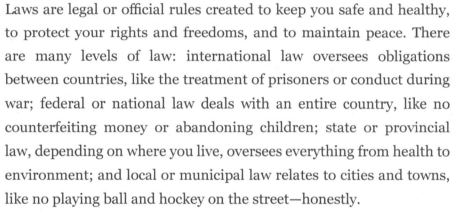

Laws are legal or official rules created to keep you safe and healthy, to protect your rights and freedoms, and to maintain peace. There are many levels of law: international law oversees obligations between countries, like the treatment of prisoners or conduct during war; federal or national law deals with an entire country, like no counterfeiting money or abandoning children; state or provincial law, depending on where you live, oversees everything from health to environment; and local or municipal law relates to cities and towns, like no playing ball and hockey on the street—honestly.

The law applies to everyone in the same way. And if laws aren't followed, you could face punishment, from doing community service, paying fines, going to jail, and even—in some countries—being sentenced to death.

EVERYDAY LIFE—AND DEATH

Flush or fine: If you don't flush a public toilet in Singapore, you can be slapped with a fine of up to one thousand Singapore dollars—and the second offence will cost you double. Be sure to have a quick look-see on your way out.

Cross your legs: Speaking of bathrooms, wait for one. In 2013, Atlanta, Georgia, became the first American state to install urine detection devices in transit station elevators to stop people from, well, peeing in the public spaces. If they do, the alarm is sounded and transit police are there in seconds. Best not to be caught with your pants down.

You can't die: Preparing for eternal rest? Think again. In 2008, the mayor of Sarpourenx, a town in France, banned the death of anyone without a reserved cemetery plot. If they did die, there would be severe punishment. (Yeah, we're not sure how that would work, either.) The reason: no more room in the local cemetery and unable to secure land to expand. The ordinance was reversed in 2010 by a new mayor. After the old mayor died. Don't worry, he had a plot reserved. A new cemetery has since been created.

HEATHER CAMLOT

And you can't be reborn: In 2007, China made it illegal for living Buddhas to reincarnate, meaning to be reborn after death, unless they receive permission from the Chinese government. Living Buddhas are high-level Tibetan monks, including the Dalai Lama, who are believed to be incarnations of Buddhist leaders. The issue stems back to the long-time struggle between China and Tibet (a self-governing region but under Chinese rule since 1951) and the question of who controls Tibetan Buddhism—and the Tibetan people.

Kooky and spooky: In 2009, a British man was sentenced to 20 weeks in jail for whistling. For more than four years, every time his neighbors came or left their residence in Wingerworth, England, he whistled the theme song to the 1960s TV show *The Addams Family*. The couple said it caused them much distress and made them feel like prisoners in their home.

ONCE UPON A TIME: Beards and moustaches were sacred in Medieval Russia. So much so that if someone damaged another person's facial hair, they'd be charged twelve grivnas, according to the 11th century code of laws known as Russkaia Pravda. For comparison's sake, if someone cut off another's finger, they would only be charged three grivnas.

Practice your handshake: If you're one for public displays of affection, you may want to cross the United Arab Emirates off your travel destinations. The code of conduct for the city of Dubai specifies that kissing out in the open is a public decency offence and could get you arrested or deported.

You're so annoying: In the Philippines, you can be jailed or fined for "unjust vexation," meaning purposefully doing something that annoys, irritates, or torments another person for no good reason, to the point of emotional distress. Keep *The Addams Family* whistling to yourself.

Till death do us start: Anyone can legally marry a dead person in France—as long as you have permission from the president and the deceased's family. French president Charles de Gaulle introduced the law in 1959 after a pregnant woman lost her fiancé when a dam burst in southern France, killing more than 400 people.

BY THE NUMBERS: 71. The number of countries/jurisdictions that consider private, consensual sexual relations between men a crime (the number is 43 for women). Maximum punishment ranges from fines and imprisonment to 100 lashes, the death penalty, and death by stoning. –*Human Dignity Trust, March 2021*

Dress to express: Expressing one's gender as something other than the one labeled at birth is a criminal act in at least 15 jurisdictions around the world and is prosecuted under laws involving "cross-dressing," "impersonation," "imitation," and "disguise."

FAMILY

(Don't) hide your pride: In 2013, Russia passed a law making it illegal to provide children under the age of 18 with information about homosexuality. The "gay propaganda" law, as it's become known, is said to protect kids' morality and health.

Hands off: All forms of corporal punishment of children—using physical force like spanking as discipline—is illegal in the home and at school in 62 countries around the world. Guess where your country stands.

Sneeze, please: Feeling under the weather? Allergies acting up? If you're in Zambia, you better not be carrying Benadryl. Non-prescription medicine with the antihistamine known as diphenhydramine is a controlled substance in the country. If caught in possession, you could be charged with drug trafficking and thrown in jail.

ONCE UPON A TIME: Throughout most of history, parents could treat their children however they pleased. Things changed in the 1870s, when 10-year-old Mary Ellen McCormack was abused so badly by her adoptive mother that the American Society for the Prevention of Cruelty to Animals stepped in. Yes, *animals*. The adoptive mother was found guilty of assault and battery, and imprisoned; Mary Ellen, after a few temporary homes, began a new life with the family of the mission worker who first came to her rescue. In 1875, The New York Society for the Prevention of Cruelty to Children, the world's first child protection service, was incorporated.

Visit your parents: In 2013, China passed the "Protection of the Rights and Interests of Elderly People" law, making it mandatory for adult children to visit their ageing parents "often" and look after their spiritual needs.

The name game: Think kids can have any name whatsoever? Think again. When a couple in 2014 decided to name their daughter Nutella—yes, like the hazelnut-chocolate spread—the judge in Valenciennes, France, overruled, saying it could lead to mockery and demeaning remarks, never mind that it's also a brand name. The judge renamed the child Ella. That's nuts!

NAMES APPROVED AND REJECTED IN NEW ZEALAND OVER THE DECADES

Approved: Talula Does the Hula From Hawaii (name changed at age 9), Violence, Number 16 Bus Shelter, Benson and Hedges (for twins)

Rejected: 4Real, Mafia No Fear, Justice, Messiah, Saint, V8, Emperor, Queen Victoria, Roman Numerals III, Lucifer, Knight, Mr. 89, 3rd, Christ, King, Anal, and names in the form of punctuation marks. —*according to CNN.com*

LIAM   EMMA   V8   OLIVIA

ANIMALS

Bowled over: Get your goldfish out of that bowl! A number of cities in Italy, including Monza in 2004 and Rome in 2005, banned round goldfish bowls after claims that they cause blindness, lack enough oxygen, and are just plain cruel. The bylaw also states that fish and other small animals can't be given away as prizes at fairs. The fish had no comment.

Stay, human, stay!: In 2004, the Italian parliament passed a law forbidding ditching Fido or Felix. And it comes with a heavy price—up to one year in jail and a fine of up to ten thousand euros. Some 80,000 cats and 50,000 dogs are abandoned every year in Italy. Many wind up on highways, cause hundreds of car accidents and deaths, and die of starvation or in collisions.

The scoop on poop: Stepping in dog poo is gross. It can also lead to some serious health hazards. That's why there are fines for people who turn a blind eye when faced with their furry friend's feces. How will anyone know, you ask? Poop detection is going high tech. Towns around the world, including in Canada, the United States, the United Kingdom, and Spain, are collecting and registering dog DNA samples. When dog droppings are found underfoot, a sample will be lifted, tested, and cross-referenced. Boom—your non-scooping days are over!

Group hug:
If you want a pet Guinea pig in Switzerland, be prepared for double the fun—and responsibility. Because Guinea pigs are social animals, the law states they must have at least one buddy for companionship. So, what do you do when one of the Guinea pigs dies and you don't want to buy another? You can rent a friend. Really.

BY THE NUMBERS: US$10 to US$23 billion. The estimated range of the annual value of international illegal wildlife trade. In terms of illegal businesses, it falls just below narcotics, human trafficking, and weapons. –*according to a report from the United Nations Environment Programme and Interpol*

Pet vacation: If you're planning a trip to Antarctica, you'd better find alternative arrangements for your furry and feathery friends. Dogs, cats, poultry, and any other non-native species cannot be brought to the southern-most continent.

Bird brain: The African grey parrot is one of the most sought-after birds because of its amazing mimicry ability and smarts. But the parrot's popularity as a pet has meant

DID YOU KNOW?
The most trafficked mammal in the world is the pangolin, which lives in Africa and Asia. Pangolin scales are valued for use in traditional Chinese medicine, while its meat is considered a delicacy.

that people have stolen the social birds right out of their wild habitat to sell them abroad, forcing the species onto the threatened list—and being declared extinct in certain countries. While the United States and the European Union banned their import in 1992 and 2007, respectively, 2016 saw the complete ban of international commercial trade. If you want an African grey parrot, make sure to get the paperwork and check that the one you are considering is captive-bred, not wild. Better yet, get two guinea pigs.

NO MORE "CAPTIVE-ATING" ACTS

It's a pretty magical moment when the circus rolls into town and you get to watch the raising of the big top. But don't expect to be entertained by wild animal acts. Many countries now have full nationwide bans:

Austria	Guatemala	Paraguay
Bolivia	Iran	Peru
Bosnia and Herzegovina	Ireland	Republic of Ireland
Colombia	Israel	Romania
Costa Rica	Italy	Scotland
Croatia	Luxembourg	Serbia
Cyprus	Macedonia	Singapore
El Salvador	Malta	Slovakia
England	Mexico	Slovenia
Estonia	The Netherlands	Wales
Greece	Norway	

—*according to Stop Circus Suffering, July 2021*

FOOD

Not-so-golden arches:
Dreaming of biting into a
Big Mac, Pepperoni P'Zone,
or Chalupa Supreme? If
you're in Bermuda, you can
keep dreaming. The island's
"Prohibited Restaurants Act 1997"
bans all international restaurant chains, including McDonalds, Pizza
Hut, and Taco Bell, in order to preserve the tourist destination's old-
world charm. You'll find only one KFC in the country, set up before
the act was passed. Go local and try the national dish: fish chowder.

Cracking up: Kinder Surprise Eggs, the chocolate eggs with a toy
inside, just can't catch a break. Chile banned them and all other
foods high in fat, sugar, salt, or calories that use a commercial hook
to sell to children under 14 years old—including toys, stickers, and
cute characters. The toys inside Kinder Surprise are why they have
been illegal in the United States since they were created in 1974. The
reason there: choking hazard. Americans can at least now crack a
Kinder Joy—sweet treat in one sealed half of the egg, toy in the other.

Hell of a smell: Some 500 students and staff were evacuated from a
university library in Melbourne, Australia, when the alarm was raised
about a possible gas leak. After firefighters searched high and low, they
traced the smell to a rotting durian fruit. Oh yes. The Southeast Asian
fruit smells like dirty gym socks *when fresh*. In another instance, the

durian fruit's odor delayed takeoff when passengers on an Indonesian plane refused to remain on board. Although flavourful and creamy, the thorny fruit is barred from some hotels, transit systems, and other enclosed spaces across the Asian continent.

Rotten to the core: Don't bother looking in stores or on menus for casu marzu—the Sardinian cheese is not allowed to be commercially made or sold. Locals on the Italian island of Sardinia have been making casu marzu cheese for centuries. The European ban was lifted because it's a traditional food, but many countries still have the delicacy on their illegal list. Why? Casu marzu, meaning "rotten cheese," is made by leaving the cheese uncovered with a slit in it so flies can lay their eggs. When the eggs hatch, maggots do their maggot thing to make the cheese all creamy. And when the cheese is ready, you eat the maggots, too. Be careful, they're jumpers!

ONCE UPON A TIME: Who'd have thunk that cute pufferfish in the 2003 movie *Finding Nemo* could be so deadly? Well, legend has it that 16th century Japanese leader Toyotomi Hideyoshi banned fugu, as it's called in Japan, after a great many of his soldiers dined on it and died. Although no longer banned today (well, except for the super toxic liver and organs), only highly trained and licensed chefs are allowed to prepare the expensive and poisonous delicacy, which, if served wrong, kills quickly—and has no known antidote.

Awesome sauce: If you want ketchup with ... well, everything, the answer is *non*! Ketchup, mayonnaise, and vinaigrette can't be offered in unlimited and/or self-serve capacity in French school cafeterias, meaning in a way that lets students drown their food in a sea of sauce. These condiments may, however, be served with select dishes. So, if French fries are on the menu, you are allowed condiments, in moderation. France's government decree is to promote healthy eating.

In hot water: Landlocked Switzerland isn't exactly known for its maritime cuisine, but that hasn't stopped the country from enacting legislation to protect lobsters and other decapods from animal cruelty—namely dropping them into a pot of boiling water while still alive. To prevent pain and suffering, lobsters must first be stunned, either by electric current or mechanical destruction of the brain, in a way that causes instant unconsciousness.

I CAN'T DO WHAT?

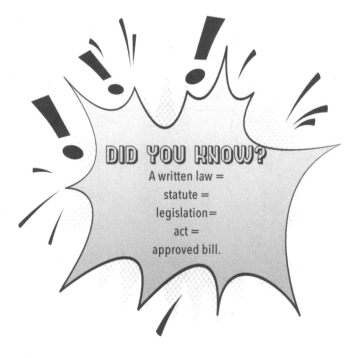

A sticky situation: Sorry to burst your bubble, but if you don't want to risk going to jail or being fined when stepping into Singapore, you'd better leave that bubble gum at home. Since 1992, it's been illegal to import and sell chewing gum (except nicotine and dental gums, which have been allowed since 2004). You can blame vandals who'd stick used chewing gum on mass transit doors, causing service disruptions, and slobs who'd leave their sticky mark on streets and sidewalks as well as in theatres, parks, and housing common areas, costing the Housing and Development Board one hundred and fifty thousand Singapore dollars a year.

DID YOU KNOW?
A written law =
statute =
legislation=
act =
approved bill.

HEATHER CAMLOT

FASHION

We gotcha covered: Hvar is a popular tourist destination, but that doesn't mean *anything goes* on the Croatian island. Enjoy the beautiful beaches, take a dip in the sea, and once you're ready to visit the historic centre, put on some clothes. Tired of rowdy and indecent behaviour, the mayor of the town of Hvar introduced some pretty hefty penalties: tourists who walk around without a shirt can be fined five hundred euros; those only in swimsuits, six hundred euros. As the town signs say, "Save your money and enjoy Hvar."

Your mask or your money: Remember the days before Covid-19? Yeah, it's not easy. During the pandemic, masks became the hot new accessory. While some countries recommended wearing them, others made them mandatory, with fines and jail time for failing to comply. The world's harshest penalty was announced in Qatar, in May 2020, when anyone outside their home without a mask could face up to three years in prison and a fine of up to two hundred thousand Qatari riyals, about US$55,000. The only exception—if you are driving alone in a vehicle.

Flip-flop flap: If you plan to walk along any of the more than 120 km (74 mi.) of hiking trails connecting the five villages of Cinque Terre, Italy, you better wear proper footwear. The paths between the cliffside villages involve some rough terrain and steep climbs, and ill-prepared hikers have had to be rescued. Flip-flops, flimsy sandals, and other smooth-soled shoes are prohibited and can get you fined up to twenty-five hundred euros!

Naked ambition: Ah, the Swiss Alps. Snow-capped peaks, fresh meadows, amazing wildlife, naked hikers. Wait, what? Soon after introducing legislation in 2009 banning naked hiking in the Swiss canton of Appenzell, a man was fined one hundred Swiss francs for trekking the mountains without wearing any clothes. His journey included passing a picnicking family and a Christian drug-rehab centre. We're still wondering whether he was wearing proper footwear.

Unmasked: Planning on buying a Jedi robe at the Star Wars: Galaxy's Edge theme park? Cool. But if you're 14 years or older, you'll have to keep it in the shopping bag. Disney Theme Parks have a strict no costumes, no masks policy for teens and adults. The reasons likely revolve around safety and brand: no one wants children to mistake an unknown costumed adult for a staff member. Caution before costume.

Veiled attack: In 2019, the Canadian province of Quebec became the first place in North America to ban religious symbols. Bill 21 makes it illegal for police officers, judges, teachers, and many others working in public sector services to wear symbols such as kippahs, hijabs, and crosses at work. The government claims such a law protects the province's secularist identity and "religious neutrality." Opponents see it as denying the rights of minorities.

Wear your Speedos: In France, you can't wear board shorts or loose swim trunks—anything that could double as street wear—in public pools for hygiene reasons. Don't even bother trying—pool attendants will jump in after you.

DID YOU KNOW?
Whether accidentally or on purpose, some clothing rules have shone a dress-code spotlight on certain minority groups. The American Civil Liberties Union, for example, has said that bans on low-riding pants target young African American men. In response, some towns have been working to annul their ordinance and end the no-sagging saga.

High and low: Hey low riders, pull 'em up! Sagging pants—low enough so others can see your skivvies or skin—can get you fined, tossed off airplanes and buses, suspended from school, ordered to do community service, and even jailed in a number of towns and cities across the United States.

A sunhat is more practical: In an act of respect for First Nations, some music festivals in Canada, England, and the United States have banned the sale of Indigenous headdresses as well as the wearing of them as fashion statements by concertgoers and artists. Show up with a culturally appropriated headdress and security will take it.

Design your own: Just because you love a pattern you saw while on vacation doesn't mean you can use it in your latest fashion collection. After a slew of foreign designers copied patterns and textiles originating from Indigenous communities in Mexico—without permission, acknowledgment, or compensation—the government approved a law in 2020 to protect these cultural works, citing a United Nations resolution on cultural rights and protection. The law makes clear that anyone plagiarizing the designs can face prison and a hefty fine. Cases of cultural theft have also arisen with the Maasai of East Africa and the Inuit of Northern Canada.

We come in peace: Heading for a beach vacation in Barbados? Leave the camouflage clothing and accessories at home. It's illegal for civilians to wear or possess the pattern as well as any part of a military uniform, past or present, from any country.

CAMO NO-NO
Antigua and Barbuda, Barbados, Dominica, Ghana, Grenada, Jamaica, Madagascar, Oman, Saint Kitts and Nevis, Saint Lucia, Saint Vincent and the Grenadines, Trinidad and Tobago, Uganda —*Government of Canada Travel Advice and Advisories*

QUIZ
MATCH THE TRAVEL ADVISORY TO ITS DESTINATION

A. Azerbaijan

B. Curaçao

C. Djibouti

D. Egypt

E. Guinea

F. Honduras

G. Iceland

H. Israel

I. Italy

J. Japan

K. Madagascar

L. Panama

M. Qatar

N. Russia

O. Tanzania

P. Thailand

Q. United Kingdom

R. United States

S. Yemen

1. Stick with a parent in the capital city. Kids wandering alone at night can be arrested if they look like they're up to no good.

2. It's illegal to say or do anything that could be offensive or insulting to the royal family.

3. You can't promote religion or try to convert people.

4. Have a tattoo? Don't be surprised if you aren't allowed at pools, beaches, hot springs, and even gyms. If you're lucky, you'll just be asked to cover up.

5. Leave your plastic bags at home—bringing them into the country and using them is not allowed.

6. Never pick up a hitchhiker before crossing the border into this country. If your new passenger is carrying anything illegal, you can get into plenty of trouble, whether you know about it or not.

7. Souvenir-shopping? Avoid the crocodile products. It's forbidden to export protected animals, including things made with them.

8. Refrain from taking pictures of police and military officers or locations.

HEATHER CAMLOT

9. No off-road driving—stay on track when in the highlands.

10. If you find a cool artifact from pre-Colonial civilizations, look but don't take. Exporting antiques and artifacts is illegal.

11. No taking pictures of the presidential palace.

12. No-drone zone. Don't bring one and don't use one or you could end up in jail.

13. Coral and conch seashells cannot be taken out of the country.

14. Hunting is illegal. Opt for animal plush toy souvenirs instead.

15. Keep your ham, bacon, and other pork products at home. Importing them is a no-no.

16. Spitting in public spaces can get you fined, while littering can land you in jail.

17. Eating and sitting on the famous church steps in the capital city can get you fined.

18. Raising your voice for something you believe in is great, but participating in an unauthorized protest in this country as a minor is illegal.

19. Keep the knives at home. Buying, selling, and/or carrying a long list of knife types is illegal.

Adapted from the Government of Canada's Travel Advice and Advisories

Answer key: 1L, 2P, 3A, 4J, 5O, 6R, 7K, 8H, 9G, 10F, 11E, 12D, 13B, 14C, 15S, 16M, 17I, 18N, 19O.

SECTION 2

SPORTS ZONE

Governing bodies of sport, like soccer's Fédération Internationale de Football Association (FIFA), the International Tennis Federation (ITF), and the National Hockey League (NHL), create the rules of the game. Without rules, there'd be no game, because no one would know or agree on how to play. These bodies also include codes of conduct—think of them as rules about behaviour, like good sportsmanship and fair play—for team members and spectators. Organizations may also regulate political statements made by players during competitions. Then there are some countries that have created codes of conduct to prevent and address maltreatment in sport, such as physical or psychological harm. If players choose not to follow the rules, they can be fined, stripped of their medals/awards, or even banned from their sport.

SOCCER

Keep your shirt on: Soccer players who take off their jerseys after scoring a goal get a cautionary yellow card (two yellow cards and you're out of the game). The International Football Association Board introduced the rule in 2004, saying the celebratory act was "unsporting behaviour" and that such "excessive displays of joy" should be avoided. With corporate logos on the front of the jerseys, we wouldn't be surprised if sponsors celebrated the rule with excessive displays of joy, knowing their brands remain front and centre when cameras zoom in on the goal scorer.

Armed to the teeth: Uruguay striker Luis Suárez received the biggest ban in World Cup history for biting Italy defender Giorgio Chiellini on the shoulder during the 2014 FIFA World Cup. That meant no playing, practicing, or entering a soccer stadium for four

HEATHER CAMLOT

months, a nine international-game suspension, and a fine of one hundred thousand Swiss francs. This was the third time Suárez had bitten someone while on the pitch!

Booting out hate: England's Chelsea Football Club has had to contend with racial and antisemitic incidents among their fans for years. Once upon a time, they simply banned the instigators from future games. But starting in 2018, the club took a new approach: through its "Say No to Antisemitism" campaign, banned fans can participate in the club's education program to understand the impact of their words and actions, and in so doing, potentially reduce their ban. Sounds pitch perfect!

Pay for play: Women's teams in Italy are attracting spectators and media coverage like never before. And yet the country's 1981 law states that these amateur teams and salaries are capped at thirty thousand euros a year. To compare, when men's star Cristiano Ronaldo played for Italy's Juventus, he earned thirty *million* euros per year. The beautiful game is in need of a makeover and the Italian Football Federation agrees: it plans to make women's soccer professional for the 2022–23 season.

Grace period: The German Football Association banned female soccer in West Germany in 1955 in order to preserve women's "grace" and to ensure their body and soul didn't suffer any harm from tough masculine game play, you know, like kicking, dribbling, passing, and heading. Ugh. The ban was lifted in 1970, and the powerhouse women would go on to win one Summer Olympics, two FIFA World Cups, and eight UEFA Champions League titles.

Ha, ha, huh?: As if the Chilean U-20 soccer team weren't upset enough about being eliminated from the 2003 South American Youth Championship in Uruguay after winning only one of their three games in the first group stage, they also got slapped with a fine. *For laughing.* The punishment came after someone told a joke while the team was eating. Higher-ups must have felt it was no time to be enjoying themselves. So much for laughing away the tears.

Change the rules = mass confusion: Organizers of the 1994 Caribbean Cup invoked an odd variation of the Golden Goal rule—if tied, the first team to score in extra time wins *and* the one goal would count as two. During the Barbados vs. Grenada game, Barbados was leading 2–1, but they needed to win by *two* goals to advance. Regular time was running out. Barbados had to act quickly. If they scored on their *own* net, they'd tie the game because the point would go to Grenada. Then they would have a chance to win in extra time. So that's what they did. Grenada, catching on, now needed to score in *either* net, but couldn't because Barbados was defending them both! The game went into extra time and Barbados scored first, winning the game 4–2.

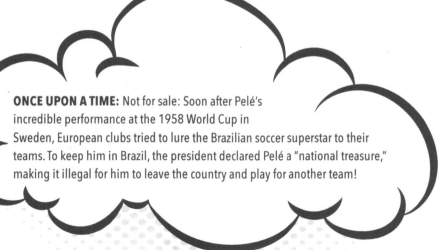

ONCE UPON A TIME: Not for sale: Soon after Pelé's incredible performance at the 1958 World Cup in Sweden, European clubs tried to lure the Brazilian soccer superstar to their teams. To keep him in Brazil, the president declared Pelé a "national treasure," making it illegal for him to leave the country and play for another team!

BASEBALL

Hot potato: Baseball is full of hidden tricks, where players try to fool a runner about the whereabouts of the ball. But in August 1987, minor league backup catcher Dave Bresnahan would go down in history for throwing a potato. Yep, a potato. Bresnahan launched the spud toward left field. The runner on third, Rick Lundblade, raced to home plate. There, he was tagged by Bresnahan, who had the ball all along. While potatoes are not specifically mentioned in the rulebook (because why would they be?), the potato prank got Lundblade the run—and got Bresnahan released from his contract.

Don't bet on it: Pete Rose, the greatest hitter of all time, was banned forever from baseball in 1989 for betting on the game that made him an American hero. Though he denied it at the time, Rose later admitted he did bet on the Cincinnati Reds—to win—while he was the team's manager. Um ... go team, go?

Bet your bottom dollar: Surprisingly, betting in baseball still goes on. Between November 2015 and March 2016, three pitchers for Japan's Yomiuri Giants were suspended indefinitely for betting on games, a fourth was suspended for a year, and three executives resigned to take responsibility. Betting on baseball, and most sports, is illegal in Japan.

And stay out: An umpire's call is the final word. But in June 1999, New York Mets manager Bobby Valentine didn't agree with a call during a Toronto Blue Jays game. He argued with the ump—and got

tossed out of the game. Valentine didn't like that either, so he changed his clothes, put on a pair of sunglasses, added a fake moustache, and returned to the dugout. Not so shockingly, the disguise didn't work, and Valentine was suspended for two games and fined US$5,000.

Deadly pitch: Cleveland Indians shortstop Ray Chapman was struck in the head and killed by a fastball thrown by New York Yankee Carl Mays in August 1920. Soon after, umpires were ordered to switch out dirty balls. Earlier that year, spitballs—baseballs that were covered in spit, tobacco juice, or other substances that caused them to fly in an unexpected way—had been banned. A spitball and dirty ball's darkened colour made them hard to see on a poorly lit, grey day—a day just like the one when Chapman was killed. Batting helmets only became mandatory in 1971.

HEATHER CAMLOT

Lucky strike: Good thing U.S. President Barack Obama was visiting Cuba on official business; otherwise, attending that March 2016 baseball game with Cuban president Raúl Castro could have been considered illegal. According to the U.S. Embassy in Cuba, there are only 12 legit reasons for Americans to travel to the island country—and tourist activities aren't among them.

Yer out: Speaking of Cuba, professional sports, including baseball, were banned in 1961 under the previous presidency of Fidel Castro (amateur competition was okay). Any Cuban player who left to play in the United States was not allowed to return home. The ban was lifted more than 50 years later.

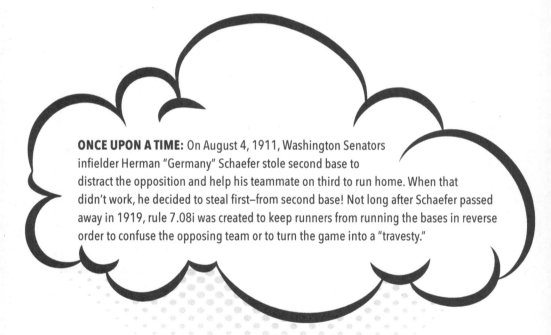

ONCE UPON A TIME: On August 4, 1911, Washington Senators infielder Herman "Germany" Schaefer stole second base to distract the opposition and help his teammate on third to run home. When that didn't work, he decided to steal first–from second base! Not long after Schaefer passed away in 1919, rule 7.08i was created to keep runners from running the bases in reverse order to confuse the opposing team or to turn the game into a "travesty."

Signed, steal-ed, and delivered: The Houston Astros won their first World Series in 2017, but that win would be tainted with a sign-stealing scandal. Just how do you steal signs, those secret, communicative hand signals and gestures between coaches and players on the field? With the centrefield camera feed. At one point, a player ran between the replay review room and the dugout with the decoded signs; at another, the bench coach contacted the review room directly; other times, texts were sent; and later, a monitor was installed near the dugout. Players relayed messages to the batter by clapping, whistling, or banging on a garbage can. The team was fined US$5 million and forfeited its first and second round draft picks in 2020 and 2021. The manager and general manager were suspended by Major League Baseball (MLB)—and fired by the Astros.

1800s BASEBALL RULES THAT NO LONGER EXIST:
- pitchers must throw underhand
- catchers stand away from the plate
- a batter is out if a fly or foul ball is caught after one bounce
- a batter can ask for a high or low pitch, and
- hitters can use a flat-sided bat. —*according to MLB.com*

ICE HOCKEY

Get out: Who knew Wayne Gretzky wasn't playing by the rules his entire career? It's true: according to the NHL rulebook, players are not allowed to tuck in their jerseys, but Gretzky famously did. The rule's got to do with appearance (numbers must be fully visible) and safety (to prevent injury like a skate blade cutting exposed skin). The rule's been around since 1964, and followed at the Olympics, but NHL refs started enforcing it in the 2013-14 season after the Great One retired.

Law of the land: Not playing by the rules of the game is one thing; not playing by the laws of the country you're in is quite another. The Canadian province of British Columbia brought criminal charges against Boston Bruin Marty McSorley for assault with a weapon. That weapon was a hockey stick, which struck Vancouver Canuck Donald Brashear in the head during a game in February 2000. Brashear collapsed, blacked out, and suffered a severe concussion. The court found McSorley guilty and offered an 18-month conditional discharge, that condition being he couldn't compete against Brashear. The NHL suspended McSorley for the rest of the season, then extended it to one full year. The veteran player never suited up for another NHL career game. Brashear retired from the NHL in 2010.

Out of sight, out of mind: Tension already runs high at games, with players shooting to win and on-edge spectators cheering their teams. You don't need to make matters worse by showing video replays on the scoreboard of anyone on the ice or in the stands challenging a ref's call, making obscene gestures, throwing objects onto the ice, or fighting with or injuring one another. Just to be sure, Russia's Kontinental Hockey League (KHL) has written these prohibitions into its rulebook. Hockey is, after all, just a game.

Reality check: In October 2010, a check from behind—an illegal hit—left 16-year-old Quebec Midget AA player Andrew Zaccardo paralyzed in his legs and with limited use of his hands and arms. In 2016, the province's superior court awarded Zaccardo and his family $8 million (US$6.2 million) in damages to be paid by the player responsible and his insurer—considered the highest Canadian payout ever for a hockey-related injury.

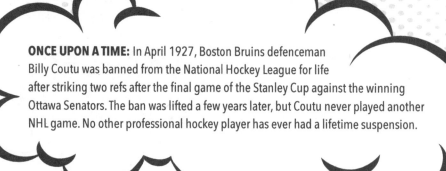

ONCE UPON A TIME: In April 1927, Boston Bruins defenceman Billy Coutu was banned from the National Hockey League for life after striking two refs after the final game of the Stanley Cup against the winning Ottawa Senators. The ban was lifted a few years later, but Coutu never played another NHL game. No other professional hockey player has ever had a lifetime suspension.

A woman's touch: European women's teams asked for body-checking to be allowed in 1990 at the first International Ice Hockey Federation-sanctioned Women's World Championship. As the North American teams didn't practice or allow it, the Europeans thought it would give them an advantage. They were very wrong. The U.S. and Canada were bigger and stronger, annihilated all the other teams, and faced each other in the final. Bodychecking was outlawed in women's hockey after the tournament—to avoid serious injury and to level the playing field! And what a playing field it is, with the spotlight on skill and speed.

Head count: Once upon a time, helmets were frowned upon and a rare sight on the ice. In January 1968, Minnesota North Stars centre Bill Masterton fell backward after being checked, hit his head on the ice, and died soon after. It was believed the 29-year-old was already suffering from an untreated concussion. Helmets became mandatory for newly signed players in 1979, a decade later. The last NHL player to take to the ice without a helmet was Craig MacTavish, who retired in 1997.

Room to groom: Don't skimp on the self-care. According to the 10-year 2013 Collective Bargaining Agreement between the NHL and the NHL Players' Association, both home and visiting players are to be provided high-quality shower products, supplies, and bath towels. Wonder what they'll ask for in their next agreement.

If at first you don't succeed: It took more than 20 years to get women's hockey in the Olympics. The first application in 1975 fizzled when many European countries cut their hockey programs because of an energy crisis. Another application went bust in 1980 when it was mistaken for field hockey. Finally, in 1992, the International Olympic Committee (IOC) announced women could hit the ice at the 1998 Olympics in Nagano, Japan—as long as the host country agreed. Japan was reluctant because it didn't have a competitive team. When Canada agreed to help coach the Japanese team, it was game on! The two countries were joined on the ice by the U.S., Finland, China, and Sweden. Gold medals all around for effort!

HEATHER CAMLOT

Singing a different tune: Okay, not a hockey rule per se, but hockey related. When the hockey team from Russia won gold at the 2018 Olympics, the players were full of pride. So much so they began singing their national anthem. What's wrong with that? The IOC had banned the Russian anthem—and the country—from the Games as punishment for previous doping violations. Some 168 Russian athletes were allowed to compete, but as neutral "Olympic Athletes from Russia" instead of Team Russia, and no national flag or anthem was allowed. The IOC was pretty forgiving of the team's excitement, though—its first gold medal in Olympic hockey since 1992.

WHAT CAN I DO?: Research the risks of bodychecking, then consider whether it should be banned in men's and boys' hockey. Why or why not?

BASKETBALL

Unbranded: A player showing up to a basketball game with a commercial logo shaved into their hair or tattooed on their body is a a no-no in the Women's National Basketball Association and NBA. Don't bother trying: in 2013, New York Knick Iman Shumpert had to shave out the three-stripe Adidas logo from his head—leaving a very obvious triangle—and in 2018, Cleveland Cavalier J.R. Smith had to tape up his calf to cover a tattoo of the Supreme clothing logo.

Running out of numbers: Unlike the WNBA and NBA, women's and men's college and high school basketball players can't sport any number that uses 6, 7, 8, or 9 on their uniform. This, according to the National Collegiate Athletic Association and The National Federation of State High School Associations. The reason: referees use both hands at once to let the scorer's table know who committed a foul, and with only five fingers per hand .... Um, can't they just watch the replay?

Get on with it: You've been awarded a free throw. It's just you, the ball, and the basket. You just have to start your routine ... and shoot that ball ... any time now ... Fact is, you don't have all the time in the world. According to the International Basketball Federation, you have five seconds (ten seconds in the United States) from the moment you catch the ball passed by the official to shooting it. Any more and you're in violation.

HEATHER CAMLOT

Watch your feet: Michael Jordan's black and red Air Ships in 1984. Athletic Propulsion Labs Concept 1 "jump enhancement" shoes in 2010. Karl-Anthony Towns's *Stranger Things* Nikes in 2016. The NBA has banned many a sneaker over the years. But it changed its policy in the 2018–19 season and welcomed all colours of the rainbow, with a few restrictions, like sharp, protruding objects and reflective material, which seems prudent. Interestingly, the WNBA had been encouraging their players to flaunt their footwear for several seasons before the NBA. We're particularly in awe of Seimone Augustus's 2018 Care Bears kicks.

"Hair must be combed neatly, braided if possible, and dressed without side-combs. A girl cannot keep her mind on the game while she is continually putting in side-combs and hair pins."

– Agnes Wayman, women's athletic coach and physical instructor, New Jersey State Normal and Model Schools, writing in 1908 about her rules on player appearance during basketball games, Spalding's Athletic Library.

Unclench that fist: Dribble, pass, shoot a basketball, sure. Punch? Uh-uh. We're not quite sure of the reason, but one guess is that using a fist makes a ball's bounce and direction unpredictable. A second guess is that it must look pretty scary watching someone run down the court with a fist. As for punching another player, that certainly falls under unsportsmanlike behaviour and will not only get a player ejected from the game, it can also result in a suspension and a fine up to US$50,000. Save the punching for boxing.

ONCE UPON A TIME: When women's basketball was created in 1892, some parents forbade their daughters from trying out because it was unladylike, what with all its running and falling and sliding and bone-breaking (not sure what they expected when playing in floor-length dresses). Doctors called for its demise because they worried about the effects on body and mind. But Senda Berenson, a gymnastics instructor at Smith College in the United States, persisted. She adapted the men's rules to "assure womanly play" by dividing the court into three zones so players wouldn't be overworked, by requiring players to hold the ball for no more than three seconds and dribble no more than three times; and by not allowing players to snatch or bat the ball from another player. The more familiar five player, full-court setup only arrived in 1971. No matter the rules, women have been on the ball for over 125 years!

For the love of it: When you're great, like Michael Jordan great, you can make certain asks. And Michael Jordan asked to play basketball in the off-season. The majority of players aren't allowed to play off-season, because clubs don't want their well-paid players risking injury. But Jordan was so passionate about the game, he asked—and got—a "love-of-the-game" clause in his first pro contract that allowed him to play anytime and anywhere.

MORE SPORTS

Signing off: You played eighteen holes, checked your card, and realized you'd just finished with the lowest score in the tournament. Congratulations! But don't start celebrating your golf victory just yet. If you don't sign that scorecard before handing it in, you can be disqualified.

Wait for it: What's with taking shirts off in sports? It's just a bad idea, as French steeplechase runner Mahiedine Mekhissi-Benabbad learned during the 2014 European Athletic Championships. On the verge of winning his third 3,000m gold medal with a nice lead, Mekhissi-Benabbad, in celebration, pulled off his shirt, gripped it in his mouth, and sailed to the finish line. He was disqualified.

DID YOU KNOW?

The International Olympic Committee allowed transgender athletes to compete for the first time at the 2004 Summer Olympic Games, as long as they met three conditions: completed gender reassignment surgery, had legal recognition of their assigned sex, and had at least two years of hormone therapy. The first Games with openly transgender athletes in competition? Tokyo 2020.

Short-comings: The women of the Norwegian beach handball team were each slapped with a one hundred and fifty euro fine by the European Handball Federation for competing in shorts rather than bikini bottoms at a 2021 European championship match. Guess what the men's teams get to wear. Go on, guess. Yep, shorts. The country's sports minister called the fine "ridiculous." With all the kerfuffle around the decision, the federation opted to donate the paid fine to an organization promoting equality in sports.

Look the part: Sure, the Olympics are about competition, but they're also about representing your country. When Japanese snowboarder Kazuhiro Kokubo showed up at the 2010 Vancouver Olympics in his official Olympic uniform with a twist—loose tie, untucked shirt, low-slung pants, as well as dreadlocks and nose piercings—the Ski Association of Japan was not impressed. Kokubo was banned from the opening ceremony. He got off lucky—the association wanted to kick him out of the Games altogether.

Mom, can I call you back?: Yes, we know how attached you are to your cellphone, but you really shouldn't have it on the tennis court. If it rings during a point, that's a "deliberate hindrance," and your opponent can stop play and claim said point. Set the phone to Do Not Disturb and leave it in your bag.

Lay down your helmet: It seems like common sense that one player can't beat up another with a helmet, and yet the National Football League (NFL) is compelled to state in its rulebook that helmets are not weapons. Wonder if Cleveland Browns defensive end Myles Garrett read that rulebook before he ripped the helmet off Pittsburgh Steelers quarterback Mason Rudolph and struck him in the head with it in November 2019. Garrett was fined US$50,000 and suspended until February 2020.

HEATHER CAMLOT

WHAT CAN I DO?: If you could add or change a rule to your favourite sport, what would it be and why?

No hankie, no thankie: If you aren't carrying a cloth handkerchief somewhere in your wrestling uniform, you aren't allowed to compete. You get one minute to find that hankie—and if you come back empty-handed, it's an automatic loss. What's the cloth for? Here's a hint: it's also called a blood rag. Yep, it's for stopping bleeding and cleaning up any bloody mess on the mat.

You can't compete until we peek: In 1966 and 1967, naked inspections, also called "nude parades," and gynecological exams of female track and field athletes were required for International Amateur Athletic Federation (now called World Athletics) events to make sure male athletes weren't cheating by competing in women's races, and to make sure females were feminine enough. Really. Ruling out unfair competition hardly makes up for the degrading and traumatic experiences women athletes had to undergo. And continue to undergo, first with chromosome testing into the 1990s and testosterone testing today.

QUIZ
MATCH THE RULE TO ITS SPORT

A. American football
B. Artistic swimming
C. Australian football
D. Boxing
E. Fencing
F. Golf
G. Polo
H. Rhythmic gymnastics
I. Shooting
J. Tennis
K. Water polo
L. Wrestling

1. Competitors cannot be perspiring as they take to the mat to begin their match.

2. If one team calls a player count for its opponents and they have more than the regulation number, the opponents will lose all points already scored that quarter.

3. Ditch the earbuds. Players can't listen to music to tune out distractions or to better their tempo.

4. Not only do competitors, coaches, officials, and spectators have to put their cellphones in silent mode, but warning signs must also be posted.

5. Opponents must salute the referee, the spectators, and each other before a bout.

6. Harlequin bottoms are forbidden in a competition outfit.

7. Players can't hide the ball under their uniform, nor can they deceive by pretending a piece of equipment is the ball.

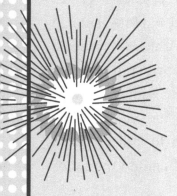

HEATHER CAMLOT

8. A player can claim a let if their opponent screams after getting stung by a bee.

9. Competitors cannot apply grease or oil to their bodies.

10. Gumshields cannot be red in whole or in part.

11. Routine competitors cannot wear theatrical makeup.

12. Players can only hold the stick with their right hand.

Adapted from each sport's rulebook.

SECTION 3

ENTERTAINMENT INTERRUPTED

Can you read, watch, listen, write, and say anything you want? According to the Universal Declaration of Human Rights, which was created in 1948 to protect the rights of every person around the world, "Everyone has the right to freedom of opinion and expression; this right includes freedom to hold opinions without interference and to seek, receive and impart information and ideas through any media and regardless of frontiers."

Yes, you can express your opinion and take in other people's opinions through books, newspapers, radio, TV, and digital media without someone stopping you. But there are some important exceptions, like spouting hate speech, writing or saying false things about a person, and copying someone else's creative work and passing it off as your own.

We've been given lot of power. Let's use it for good, not evil.

BOOKS AND MEDIA

Hate for Harry: The Harry Potter series contained the most banned/challenged books between 2000 and 2009 in the United States, for their use of magic, witchcraft, violence, and a whole lot of spells. Harry obviously incanted the vanishing spell "evanesco" to get the books wiped off the next decade's list, but some popular favourites for the American Library Association's 2010 to 2019 list of banned/challenged titles include Dav Pilkey's *Captain Underpants*, Raina Telgemeier's *Drama*, Angie Thomas's *The Hate U Give*, and topping the list, *The Absolutely True Diary of a Part-Time Indian* by Sherman Alexie. Wonder if "evanesco" would work for them, too.

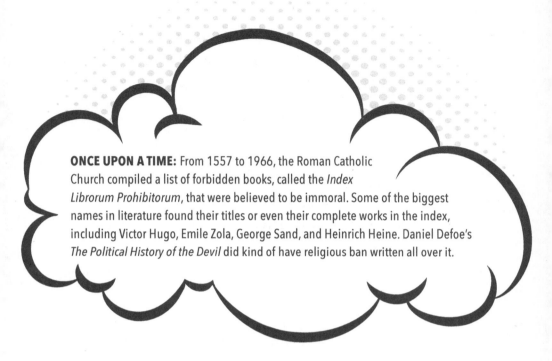

ONCE UPON A TIME: From 1557 to 1966, the Roman Catholic Church compiled a list of forbidden books, called the *Index Librorum Prohibitorum*, that were believed to be immoral. Some of the biggest names in literature found their titles or even their complete works in the index, including Victor Hugo, Emile Zola, George Sand, and Heinrich Heine. Daniel Defoe's *The Political History of the Devil* did kind of have religious ban written all over it.

Comic cleanse: Corrupting our youth! Turning teens into juvenile delinquents! By the late 1930s, the United States saw the start of a much-heated debate about comics. Comics went up in flames at book burnings in the 1940s and went on trial in the 1950s, leading to the Comics Code Authority, a self-censorship unit created by the comics industry. Cities and states passed their own laws, too. Soon horror, crime, and sci-fi comics were zapped and the rest washed clean, with good always triumphing over evil. The code was revised a couple of times, but lost its edge with the emergence of comic book stores, independent publishers, and the desire for more creativity in the pages. The code lasted until 2011.

Exiled and executed: An Iranian journalist living in exile in France, who had reported on Iran's anti-government protests in 2017 and 2018, was arrested while in Iraq. Ruhollah Zam was then taken to Iran and tried on accusations of spreading information about the protests and inciting violence. Zam, who ran the anti-government news site AmadNews, was found guilty of "corruption on earth" and sentenced to death. He was hanged in December 2020.

There's no denying it: Remember the part about using your power for good, not evil? You actually can't just write or say anything. In Germany, publishing pro-Nazi materials and hate speech online and offline is against the law. Similarly, it's illegal in more than a dozen European Union countries as well as in Israel to say the Holocaust never happened.

Private eyes: In 2013, Malala Yousafzai's memoir, *I Am Malala: The Girl Who Stood Up for Education and Was Shot by the Taliban*, co-written by Christina Lamb, was banned in more than 100,000 private schools in her home country of Pakistan for not showing enough respect for Islam. She was called a tool of the West.

TOP 10 COUNTRIES THAT CENSOR INDEPENDENT MEDIA. METHODS RANGE FROM JAILING JOURNALISTS TO RESTRICTING INTERNET ACCESS: Eritrea, North Korea, Turkmenistan, Saudi Arabia, China, Vietnam, Iran, Equatorial Guinea, Belarus, Cuba.
—Committee to Protect Journalists, February 2021

Clothes call: In January 1942, Wonder Woman graced the cover of the first *Sensation Comics*. Two months later, the publication was blacklisted by the U.S. National Organization for Decent Literature and added to its list of "Publications Disapproved for Youth." The reason: with her red bustier and knee-high boots, blue-and-white-starred culottes, and gold tiara, Wonder Woman wasn't "sufficiently dressed."

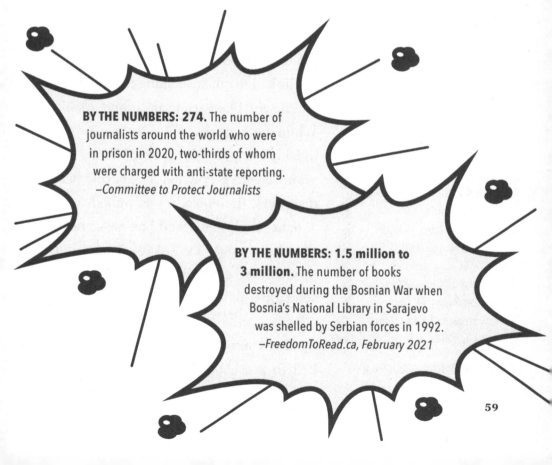

WHAT CAN I DO?: Look around. Have you seen evidence of hate speech in social media or on television? Consider whether the perpetrator should be punished. If so, how? If not, why not?

Indecent exposure:

Winnie-the-Pooh may be a beloved children's icon, but officials in the town of Tuszyn, Poland, refused to consider the silly old bear as a playground mascot in 2014 due to his lack of pants and unclear gender. They later claimed it was a joke that got out of hand. Uh-huh. Wonder if they considered Donald Duck or Squidward. Oh, wait, never mind.

BY THE NUMBERS: 274. The number of journalists around the world who were in prison in 2020, two-thirds of whom were charged with anti-state reporting. –*Committee to Protect Journalists*

BY THE NUMBERS: 1.5 million to 3 million. The number of books destroyed during the Bosnian War when Bosnia's National Library in Sarajevo was shelled by Serbian forces in 1992. –*FreedomToRead.ca, February 2021*

FILM AND TELEVISION

Abominable abomination: How does *Abominable*, a feel-good DreamWorks animated movie, get banned in several Asian countries? By including a controversial map of the South China Sea that was declared invalid by the Permanent Court of Arbitration in The Hague. The map has a nine-dash line around the waters and islands that China claims as its own—parts of which are claimed by other Asian countries. Vietnam, Malaysia, and the Philippines refused to screen the 2019 film, a U.S.–China co-production.

Anime attack: After watching the *Pokémon* episode "Dennō Senshi Porygon" on December 16, 1997, more than 600 children in Japan were rushed to hospital with symptoms ranging from headaches and dizziness to blurred vision and seizures. The health crisis, dubbed "Pokémon shock," was linked to quick-flashing red and blue lights, like strobe lights, when Pikachu blasted a thunderbolt attack. While the majority of viewers recovered quickly (a few discovered they had photosensitive epilepsy, a neurological disorder), the episode was pulled from Japanese television and has never been broadcast since. TV Tokyo also set out production guidelines for animation soon after.

10 DISNEY ANIMATED FILMS WITH CHARACTERS WHO SMOKE:
101 Dalmatians, Aladdin, Alice in Wonderland, Dumbo, Hercules, Peter Pan, Pinocchio, The Great Mouse Detective, The Hunchback of Notre Dame, The Little Mermaid

Spiders are not your friends: The British preschool cartoon *Peppa Pig* is chock-full of positive messages, unless you live in Australia. In the episode "Mister Skinny Legs," Peppa's dad tells her that spiders are small and can't hurt her, so she befriends the eight-legged guest in her home. But in Australia, spiders can be large, dangerous, and deadly—we're looking at you, Mister Funnel-web. The episode was twice pulled from viewing, first by the Australian Broadcasting Corporation in 2012, and again by payTV channel Nick Jr. in 2017.

E.T. go home: In a decision backed by child psychologists, Sweden, Finland, and Norway banned kids from seeing the 1982 sci-fi epic *E.T.: The Extra-Terrestrial* during its original release because adults came across as children's enemies. In Sweden, if you wanted to see the movie, you had to be 11+, Finland, 8+, and Norway, 12+. Children were so unhappy about being told they couldn't see a kids' movie (because, why wouldn't they be?!) that they took to the street in protest.

Tooned out: In June 2017, the Kenya Film Classification Board banned six American TV cartoons because it concluded the messages within them had an LGBT "agenda" and glorified "deviant behaviour." The programs: *Loud House, The Legend of Korra, Hey Arnold!, Clarence, Steven Universe,* and *Adventure Time.* Homosexuality is illegal in Kenya, and content introducing it to children, the KFCB said, is forbidden.

Salut Netflix: In 2017, Netflix had two films in competition at the Cannes Film Festival, but French filmmakers complained about the streaming giant as its films never played in theatres. In response, the prestigious festival added a new rule for 2018: films eligible for competition must be theatrically released in France. The thing is, Netflix is a service watched pretty much at home and *not* in theatres. If Netflix followed the Cannes rule, its movies wouldn't be seen in French homes until three years later. Why? Because French law says a film can't be shown on a streaming platform until 36 months after its theatre run. Netflix could show its films at Cannes out of competition, but as of 2021, that had yet to happen.

Silenced superhero: *Wonder Woman* was banned by Lebanon just before the film was set to premiere there. The reason: Israeli star Gal Gadot. Lebanon and Israel have technically been at war for many, many years and although they're in a ceasefire, the country still bans contact with Israelis and travel to Israel, and boycotts Israeli products. *Wonder Woman* was one of the Top 10 highest grossing films of 2017.

Lift a finger or three: Thailand's military leaders banned the three-finger salute from the movie and book franchise *The Hunger Games*

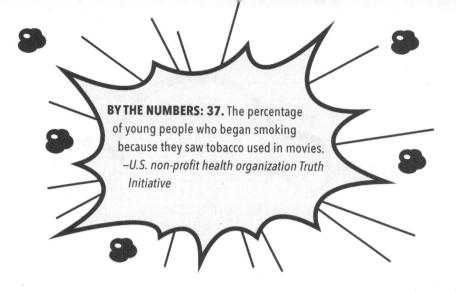

BY THE NUMBERS: 37. The percentage of young people who began smoking because they saw tobacco used in movies. –*U.S. non-profit health organization Truth Initiative*

in 2014. The film's salute, a sign of resistance against totalitarian rule, gained popularity in Thailand as a silent symbol of protest and defiance against the military coup. The salute has spread over the years and throughout the world—protesters flashed three fingers in Myanmar in early 2021 after a military coup in that country.

Put it out: You won't be seeing as much smoking in your favourite TV shows and movies these days. Since 2004, studios have been adding cigarette- and e-cigarette-free policies for their youth programming—meaning TV-14 shows and PG-13 films and under—in an attempt to keep kids from picking up the unhealthy habit. While the preference is for characters not to be smoking at all, there is leeway for historical accuracy and substantial "creative" reasons.

The capital of Communism?: The House Un-American Activities Committee probably means nothing to you, but back in the 1940s and 1950s, HUAC was feared and despised in the U.S. movie capital. The committee was on a witch hunt for Communists and believed the film industry was full of them. HUAC called in actors, writers,

ONCE UPON A TIME: No big screen for little people. In 1928, children under 16 years old were banned from movie theatres in Quebec, Canada, after 78 people, most of them children, died during a fire in the city of Montreal's Laurier Palace in 1927. The name of the movie: *Get 'Em Young.* The ban remained until 1961.

directors, musicians, and more to testify about whether they were Communists, and to name suspected Communists. If they didn't cooperate, they could be sentenced to prison. Meanwhile, studios refused to hire, i.e., "blacklisted," the supposed and suspected Communists to stay on HUAC's good side. We're talking more than 300 of the day's biggest stars, like Charlie Chaplin, Lena Horne, and Orson Welles. Many careers were ruined, though some were lucky enough to recover come the 1960s.

Seven dirty words: The 1972 comedy routine "Seven Words You Can Never Say on Television" led to a historic U.S. Supreme Court case on free speech and censorship on television and radio. When "Filthy Words," a 1973 version of comedian George Carlin's Seven

Words monologue, aired on radio at 2 PM, a listener—with his 15-year-old son at the time—complained. After a years-long battle, the Federal Communications Commission won the case against station owner Pacifica Foundation. The court stated the FCC has the right to restrict indecent language at certain times of the day because of radio and television's accessibility to children (cable channels don't have the same rules). That's why you still won't hear those seven dirty words on broadcast radio and television today— nor will we repeat them here!

MUSIC AND DANCE

No "Happy" dance: In 2014, a group of young Iranians were sentenced to six months to one year in jail and 91 lashes for a viral video they created to Pharrell Williams's song "Happy." Their sentences were suspended, but the law remains in Iran: women cannot dance in public or appear without headscarves, and there is no dancing with the opposite sex.

Contra-alto: A whites-only policy denied Black classical singer Marian Anderson the opportunity to perform for her fans and admirers at Constitution Hall in Washington, D.C., in April 1939. The owners of the hall then and now are the Daughters of the American Revolution, an exclusive organization whose all-female members are descendants of revolutionary patriots. But that policy didn't stop the world-renowned Anderson from singing. Instead, she performed outside, at Washington's Lincoln Memorial—to an audience of 75,000! The concert proved pivotal in U.S. civil rights history, and remains one of the century's greatest musical moments.

Hit play: Pop stars aren't like the rest of us, at least in South Korea. In December 2020, a new law was passed allowing top K-pop stars who meet specific criteria to defer their mandatory military service, which begins no later than age 28. The law came into effect days before the oldest member of the award-winning and internationally renowned boyband BTS turned 28. Before the "BTS law," as it's being called, only certain people could opt out, like classical musicians and top athletes. With BTS boosting South Korea's reputation and breaking records across the globe, the new law seems like a nice way to say thank you. BTS's army of fans are no doubt delighted.

Silent nights: A good party always has good music, but according to recent laws in the region of Calvià, Spain, which includes party destination Magaluf, that music can't be louder than 60 decibels—about the level of normal conversation—in bars and restaurants. At night, the sound can't exceed 35 decibels—between a soft whisper and a refrigerator hum. Businesses had to install sound limiters, which cut in at the appropriate levels. The town says the penalties, including fines up to twelve thousand euros and music activity suspensions, are to protect local residents and to create a more family-friendly destination.

10 REASONS WHY SONGS HAVE BEEN BANNED OR CENSORED ACROSS THE GLOBE: Profanity, sexual references, drug references, politics, violence, blasphemy/religious references, morbid content, sensitivity to recent situation (such as lyrics with death and destruction during wartime), brand-name marketing, and stuttering (yes, really).
—*The National Coalition Against Censorship*

Non-teaching moment: There are many reasons why songs may be banned, but insulting teachers isn't usually one of them. However, in 2017, Cambodia's Ministry of Information informed radio and TV stations that they were to stop playing *"Kru bong rien srovoeung sra,"* or "Drunk Teacher," by singer Chen Sai Chai, because it insulted the profession. Songwriter Yem Tasrong said the lyrics refer to one single teacher and reflect his experience. A year earlier, the ministry banned a rap song about school boredom and how to skip out of class.

CanCon conquerers: To promote Canadian artists, 35 percent of the music played on Canadian radio must be Canadian content, meaning at least two of four requirements must be met. In simplest terms, the music must be composed by a Canadian, the lyrics written by a Canadian, the music or lyrics performed by a Canadian, or a live performance recorded or performed and broadcast in Canada. That's why you hear so much Shawn Mendes and Drake on Canadian radio!

ONCE UPON A TIME: *Joik* is one of Europe's oldest forms of music, but for centuries it was pushed underground and even banned. The traditional vocal melodies of the Sami, an Indigenous people of northern Scandinavia, were considered sinful and outlawed by Christian missionaries in the 17th century, along with the persecution of Sami culture, traditions, and religion. The efforts to assimilate the Sami into European society continued through the 1950s, and governments forbade *joik* in school settings. Fortunately, *joik* has returned over the past few decades–so much so that it can be heard in the opening scene of the 2013 Disney film *Frozen* as well as at the Eurovision Song Contest 2019.

Music to move: South African singer Miriam Makeba lived in exile for three decades because of her criticism of apartheid through her songs, a documentary film, as well as a speech she made at the United Nations. Apartheid was a system established by the white minority rule to segregate by race. South Africa banned Makeba's music and revoked her citizenship and passport. Even so, she continued to speak up and sing out against the regime and for hope for a better and equal future. "Mama Africa," as the world-famous singer was known, only returned home in 1990, when apartheid was no more.

Behind the name: One of Mexico's most popular norteño bands, Los Tucanes de Tijuana, is banned from the town of Tijuana because the lead singer once sent his regards to two drug lords while onstage. Some of the band's songs are also banned in parts of Mexico—those that are of the subgenre known as narcocorridos, which tell the very real stories of the country's drug cartels. Don't feel too badly for Los Tucanes de Tijuana though: the award-winners hit the stage at California's Coachella—one of the biggest music festivals in the world—and got the key to the fest city in 2019.

7 DANCES THAT WERE ONCE BANNED FOR INDECENT, RELIGIOUS, POLITICAL, OR EVEN HEALTH REASONS:

Dance name, place it was banned, approximate first year it was banned.

Hula – Hawaii, 1830

Batuque – Portugal, 1866

Plains Indigenous Sun Dance – Canada, 1895

Bharatanatyam – India, 1910

Animal Dances (Turkey Trot, Bunny Hug, Grizzly Bear ...) – United States, 1909

Sema – Turkey, 1925

Apsara – Cambodia, 1975

HEATHER CAMLOT

TECHNOLOGY

Blame the games: After two shootings at U.S. Walmart stores during the summer of 2019, the mega-retailer asked employees to remove signs and displays of violent video games. Although it would have made it harder to spot the games—which psychologists have continually said are not linked to violent behaviour—shoppers could still buy them. Oh, and you could still buy guns at many American Walmart stores.

An eye sore: If you have a laser pointer, even a toy with a laser pointer, it may be *verboten* in Switzerland. The country has banned all lasers over the smallest classification of 1. Class 1 is like the enclosed laser in a CD or DVD player, and is considered the only level that is absolutely safe. The reason for the ban: the level of radiation in a laser-beam can cause eye damage, from short-term irritation to blindness, never mind disturbing drivers and pilots. Just point your finger—it's better to be rude than dangerous.

BY THE NUMBERS: 71. The percentage of Internet users living in countries where people have been arrested or sent to prison for writing political, social, or religious commentary online. –*Freedom on the Net 2019 Report by Freedom House*

ONCE UPON A TIME: In 1976, a new arcade game hit the floors and set off a moral panic, leading to its being pulled from some arcades and an amusement park, and even dropped by a distributor. The black and white "Death Race" involved players behind the wheel trying to run down gremlins, which looked eerily like stick-figure people. Upon impact, a shriek would sound and a grave marker would appear. The game, whose cabinet was covered in grim reapers and gravestones, was described as "macabre" and "morbid"—and led to a spike in sales.

Game plan: In an attempt to cut video game addiction and the mental and physical health issues that come from it, China set a curfew and time limit in 2019 for online gamers under 18 years old. That ban took place between 10 PM and 8 AM and limited playing time to one and a half hours during the weekday and three hours on weekends and public holidays. As of fall 2021, gaming became even more restrictive: a full ban from Monday to Thursday, and a partial ban on Fridays, Saturdays, Sundays, and public holidays, when gaming is allowed between the hours of 8 PM and 9 PM only. China is right to be concerned: the World Health Organization added "gaming disorder"—major video-game addiction—to its International Classification of Diseases, making it a serious health issue.

Player terminated: Cheat in Pokémon GO and you're out. Those rules (yes, there are rules) for the mobile game specifically state that cheating includes falsifying your location, trading accounts, and sharing accounts, among others. You get two chances to mend your ways. Third time—game over.

High energy: There are lots of reasons video games are banned: violence, gore, and sexual content are top of mind. But back in 2010—a lifetime ago in the video game world—Denmark banned EA Sports MMA (mixed martial arts) for a much different reason. Can you guess? Bet you can't. Energy drinks. Yep, laws in Denmark don't allow energy-drink marketing, and the video game features precisely that. EA Sports opted not to alter the in-game advertised products and let it be banned.

Run for your life: If you're going to run with the bulls during Spain's annual festivity, do not take a selfie. Nope, not a photo or a video. The city of Pamplona banned any self-documenting adventures, and police will hunt you down and fine you if you do—that is, if you haven't been killed by the bull first. No joke—death and injury are very real possibilities, even without a smartphone in hand.

Social media showdown: Student-favourite research site Wikipedia was banned in Turkey in April 2017. The government asked the online encyclopedia to remove content criticizing the government. When Wikipedia refused, the country followed its rule of law, claiming threats to national security, and stopped access. Wikipedia was unblocked in January 2020, after the ban was ruled a violation of freedom of expression by the country's top constitutional court. Over the years, Turkey has blocked various websites and arrested journalists, human rights activists, and others for criticizing the government over social media.

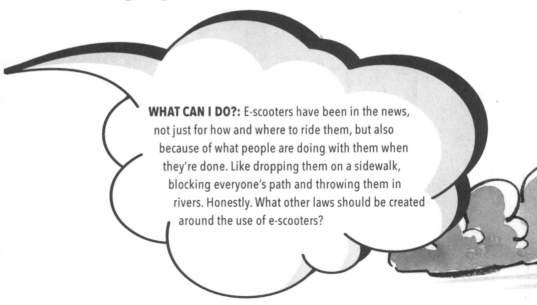

WHAT CAN I DO?: E-scooters have been in the news, not just for how and where to ride them, but also because of what people are doing with them when they're done. Like dropping them on a sidewalk, blocking everyone's path and throwing them in rivers. Honestly. What other laws should be created around the use of e-scooters?

Not fake news: The Donald Trump presidency came to an end in 2021, but not before his Twitter account did. The social media giant banned the president for life, stating that Tweets he made broke the platform's policy relating to the glorification of violence. The announcement came after the storming of the U.S. Capitol on January 6, 2021. Some called the ban censorship and a violation of free speech, but Twitter defended its move as in the interest of public safety. At the time of writing, Snapchat had also permanently banned Trump.

Scoot over: E-scooters are popping up all around the world, but you can't just ride them as you please. New laws are coming into effect all the time, especially as deaths and accidents rise. While some countries ban e-scooters from sidewalks, cycle paths, and/or public roads, others have minimum age requirements and speed limits.

Time's up: Members of the U.S. Army and Navy are banned from using the video-sharing app TikTok on their government-issued mobile devices. Officials believe the Chinese app is a security threat and could be used for spying or collecting personal information. Interestingly, the Army was using TikTok for its own recruitment.

Watch over and out: Talk about invasion of privacy. It seems some German parents have been secretly listening in on conversations between their child and their teacher ... through a smartwatch. The SIM-card-carrying watches are marketed for children and can be enabled via an app. But any transmission or telecommunications system that is masked as something else—in this case a watch—and allows others to unknowingly listen in is against the law. Not only do the spy-like watches have to be destroyed by consumers, but those consumers also have to provide proof the smartwatches were destroyed.

HEATHER CAMLOT

TOP 10 COUNTRIES WITH THE LEAST INTERNET AND DIGITAL MEDIA FREEDOM:

Based on limits on content (like blocking websites), obstacles to access (like economic barriers), and violations of user rights (like imprisonment for what people do or say online).

China

Cuba

Iran

Syria

Vietnam

Sudan

Egypt

Saudi Arabia

Uzbekistan

Pakistan

—*Freedom on the Net 2019 Report by Freedom House*

I CAN'T DO WHAT?

QUIZ
MATCH THE BOOK TO THE REASON IT WAS BANNED OR CHALLENGED

1. *And Tango Makes Three* by Peter Parnell and Justin Richardson
2. *Alice in Wonderland* by Lewis Carroll
3. *Barefoot Gen* by Keiji Nakazawa
4. *Brave New World* by Aldous Huxley
5. *Drama* by Raina Telgemeier
6. *Green Eggs and Ham* by Dr. Seuss
7. *Little Blue and Little Yellow* by Leo Lionni
8. *Persepolis* by Marjane Satrapi
9. *The Complete Fairy Tales* by the Brothers Grimm
10. *The Diary of a Young Girl* by Anne Frank
11. *The Hate U Give* by Angie Thomas
12. *The Story of Ferdinand* by Munro Leaf
13. *The Tale of Peter Rabbit* and *Benjamin Bunny* by Beatrix Potter
14. *The Waiting Dog* by Carolyn Beck and Andrea Beck
15. *Tintin in the Congo* by Hergé
16. *7 Generations: A Plains Cree Saga* by David Alexander Robertson

Answer key: 1L, 2E, 3P, 4G, 5J, 6H, 7N, 8K, 9A, 10D, 11I, 12F, 13B, 14C, 15M, 16O

78

A. Banned by Allied forces claiming the book depicted the roots of Nazism (Germany, around 1945).

B. Opposed by an English county council that had issue with the "middle-class rabbits" (England, 1980s).

C. Called "revolting" and "vile" by a parent in Ontario (Canada, 2006).

D. Called "a real downer" by the Alabama State Textbook Committee (U.S., 1983).

E. Banned by the governor of Hunan Province because the animals use human language and are on the same level as humans (China, 1931).

F. Banned by the government for pacifist propaganda (Spain, 1938).

G. Banned upon release for being anti-religion and anti-traditional family (Ireland, 1932).

H. Banned for commentary on Marxism (China, 1965).

I. Challenged for being anti-cop by the Fraternal Order of Police in South Carolina (U.S., 2018).

J. Repeatedly challenged for containing LGBTQIA+ characters and themes (U.S., 2014).

K. Condemned for being Islamophobic (Iran, early 2000s).

L. Challenged and later banned for depicting same-sex parents (U.S., starting in 2006).

M. Taken to court for racist content (Belgium, 2010).

N. Called a potential threat to traditional family values by a Venice mayor (Italy, 2015).

O. Placed on a "Books to Weed Out" list by Edmonton Public Schools due to its sensitive subject matter, such as the abuse at residential schools (Canada, 2018).

P. Pulled by a couple of Japanese cities for being too graphic and/or for potentially discriminatory language (Japan, 2013 and 2014).

SECTION 4

KID CONCERNS

Raise your hand before asking the teacher a question. Wait for the bell to ring before leaving class. Don't pick a toy that's marked 12+ when you're only eight. When you're a kid, it seems like there are a lot of rules all for one reason: to keep you from having any fun.

You know that's not really why there are rules. Imagine the chaos in the classroom with everyone leaving whenever they wanted to— learning would be impossible. And a toy in the wrong hands? That can lead to potential choking hazards, or worse.

Along with rules in school and about toy safety, children have a very special set of rules just for them. These rules, called rights, are set out in the United Nations Convention on the Rights of the Child, which almost every country in the world has signed and agreed to follow. These rights, which are protected by law, include the right to life, to play, and to an education as well as to be protected from violence, abuse, and neglect.

Pretty important stuff, those rules.

SCHOOL

What's left?: Schools have so many clothing policies, it's hard to figure out what a student can actually wear. While some rules were created to make all students feel welcome, others are doing the opposite, by pushing gender stereotypes and pointing out that certain clothing distracts boys during their studies. Ummm, seriously? So, what are some of the offensive items? It all depends on where you live and the school you attend, but they include leggings, tights, yoga pants, skinny jeans, saggy pants, short shorts, mini-skirts, uniform skirts, pants worn by female students during graduation and prom, tank tops, crop tops, ripped jeans, hats, not to mention hair extensions, makeup, and earrings.

Back-to-school shopping: Schools around the world are in the throes of banning knapsacks for health and safety reasons—think hitting someone in the halls accidentally or causing back strain from being overloaded. But the state of Louisiana in the United States has written into law that students *can* wear backpacks—of the bulletproof kind. Scary.

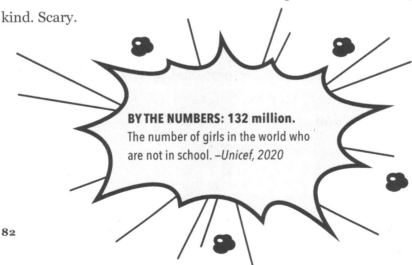

BY THE NUMBERS: 132 million. The number of girls in the world who are not in school. –*Unicef, 2020*

Don't ever go there: There is no such thing as Holocaust humour. Period. In 2019, a British teacher told students that if they didn't wrap up their work fast enough, they would be sent to the gas chambers. More than a third of the students in the elementary school class in Radlett, England, were Jewish. When challenged, the teacher tried covering up by saying it was a joke and by apologizing, then asking the kids not to repeat the comment. They did repeat the comment— and the school fired her, fast.

Hands down: Some North American schools have implemented no hugging, no touching, no loving policies—between students (years before COVID-19 arrived). The rules put the kibosh on tag, hand-holding, and a supportive pat on the back. Some claim it's for sexual harassment reasons, others for safety, and still others for learning to respect personal space. Human connection has been disconnected.

1 + 2 = 3 little pigs: In 2014, Russia's Education and Science Ministry barred a popular math textbook written by educator Lyudmila Peterson because it included foreign characters like Snow White and the Seven Dwarfs that weren't representative of Russian culture and didn't instil patriotism.

Make a mess: You can make all the mess you want, but if you're a student in Japan, you'll likely be cleaning it up, too. From tidying classrooms to wiping handrails to making toilets sparkle, students take care of basic school cleanup as part of their education. The routine helps to build character, strengthen teamwork, develop pride in their surroundings, and fosters responsible members of society.

With child, without education: As president, John Magufuli had made it very clear that pregnant girls in Tanzania were forbidden to attend school. And once they gave birth, the teenagers still couldn't return. Tanzania has one of the highest teen pregnancy rates in the world at 27 percent, and in the past 10 years, some 55,000 pregnant girls have been expelled. In November 2020, the law was being challenged in court. In March 2021, Magufuli died. Soon after, the country created an alternative education program but hadn't budged on mainstream schooling. In the meantime, maybe the state should question why teen pregnancy is so high.

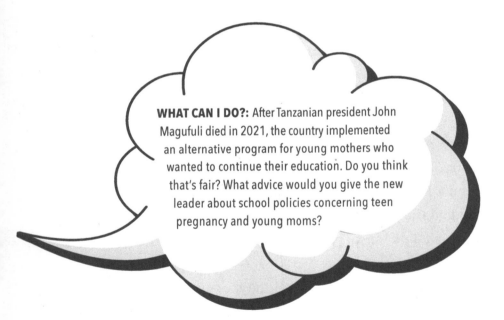

WHAT CAN I DO?: After Tanzanian president John Magufuli died in 2021, the country implemented an alternative program for young mothers who wanted to continue their education. Do you think that's fair? What advice would you give the new leader about school policies concerning teen pregnancy and young moms?

HEATHER CAMLOT

DID YOU KNOW? The first residential school in Canada opened in 1831 with the purpose of educating and integrating Indigenous children into white, Christian society. In 1920, attendance became mandatory for all seven- to fifteen-year-old Indigenous children, who were forced from their homes and their families, severely punished for speaking their language and practicing their traditions, and given new names, clothes, and haircuts in order to "civilize" them. Run by Christian churches and set up by the government, more than 130 residential schools opened with some 150,000 children, most of whom suffered physical, sexual, and emotional abuse as well as malnutrition and rampant disease at the schools. When the last school closed in 1996, more than 4,000 Indigenous children had died and thousands more were never heard from again.

WHAT CAN I DO?: To help build the path toward reconciliation, read the youth-friendly "Spirit Bear's Guide to the Truth and Reconciliation Commission of Canada Calls to Action" in the educational resources section at FNcaringsociety.com. To understand international Indigenous rights, read "Know Your Rights! United Nations Declaration on the Rights of Indigenous Peoples for Indigenous Adolescents" at Unicef.org.

Going green: Has a big red X on a test or assignment made you feel like a big old failure? Well, some school administrators think so and have banned real-angry red for marking. Yup, teachers in classrooms from England to India to Australia are turning to go-for-it green and pat-on-the-back pink. You're still marked wrong for mistakes, but at least they look prettier.

HEATHER CAMLOT

TOYS

Weapon of mini destruction: In 2017, a new toy in China had provinces across the country banning it and police raiding shops to seize it. The mini toothpick crossbow was less toy and more weapon—the toothpick could pierce apples, cardboard, and balloons. The crossbow could also be loaded with even more dangerous replacements, like needles and nails. One YouTube video showed a mini crossbow loaded with a steel bolt—shattering a lightbulb and punching a hole in a can of soda. Who thinks this stuff up?

Too hot to handle: In 2007, Hasbro recalled a million pink and purple Easy-Bake Ovens after receiving more than 70 reports of varying burns when children got their fingers caught in the oven's opening. One five-year-old girl had to have a finger partially amputated after suffering a serious burn. The oven was first introduced in 1963 and used an incandescent lightbulb—until its 2011 remake—to bake mini cakes and cookies.

WHAT CAN I DO?: Write a list of regulations and safety tests you think toy companies should live by.

Finger food: Stop feeding that doll! Cabbage Patch Kids were all the rage in the 1980s and continue to sell today. But in early 1997, Mattel hit a sour patch when some of its Snacktime Kids dolls took their snacking to the extreme by sampling children's hair and fingers. The company quickly pulled the dolls from store shelves, discontinued the product, and offered a voluntary full cash refund for the approximately 500,000 dolls sold.

HEATHER CAMLOT

Water warning: Yo-yo water balls were flung onto the market in the early 2000s, and soon countries from Canada to Brazil, Luxembourg to Australia were banning the toy for risk of strangulation as reports came in of incidents from eye injuries to suffocation. The liquid-filled ball attaches to a finger loop via a long stretchy cord that could not only wrap itself around a child's neck when stretched, but could also stick together because of the rubbery material. And then there were the models that lit up and whose batteries could fall out, leading to choking and major damage to the esophagus.

Choo-chew: Do all young children go through a Thomas the Tank Engine phase? Possibly. Do they eat their trains and accessories? Possibly. That's why, in 2007, a slew of Thomas & Friends Wooden Railway Toys made in China were recalled. Their paint contained lead, which could lead to poisoning and serious health problems. The recall involved some 1.5 million toys.

Watch and learn: Do grown-ups take kids' toys to work? The U.S. National Security Agency had such worries in 1999 that it issued a memo to staff, banning Furbys from its Maryland premises because the spy agency believed the talking Furby could record conversations, and as such, repeat classified information outside its walls. The toy company said that while the toy was clever, Furbys had no recording capabilities.

Go directly to jail: Monopoly is all about capitalism—buying properties and building all those houses and hotels. Which is pretty much why Cuba's communist leader Fidel Castro banned the board game and ordered all sets destroyed when he came to power in 1959.

Brick trick: You can build a lot of things with Lego bricks, but if you're going to build a replica machine gun and hold it in front of a window, then you shouldn't be surprised when the police show up at your door and place you under investigation for possible weapons law violations. Which is what happened in Ludwigshafen, Germany, in 2018, when a 19-year-old played with his realistic-looking, yet plastic, creation by his apartment window.

Spin doctor: They were marketed to help children with autism, ADHD, and anxiety, but fidget spinners took the world by storm in 2017, much to the ire of teachers. Soon enough, the hot new thing was being confiscated and banned in classrooms, and wound up on the European Union's list of dangerous products—specifically those with batteries and detachable parts.

ONCE UPON A TIME: In 1933, Syria banned the yo-yo. The up and down toy, a recent release in the country, was blamed for the terrible drought that was killing cattle. Religious chiefs claimed the yo-yo's upswing toyed with prayers for a downpour of rain. Yo-yos were immediately confiscated.

Step away from the radiation, kid: In 1950, what is probably the most dangerous toy in the world, was released. The Gilbert U-238 Atomic Energy Lab came complete with radioactive ores, three additional radiation sources, a Geiger counter, a cloud chamber, a booklet on how to prospect for uranium, and more. The box boasted the kit was "Exciting!" and "Safe!" But people had their doubts. If it wasn't the radioactivity that made a parent stop and think, the price tag certainly did. At US$50—about US$500 in today's dollars—it was way too steep for a children's toy. The Gilbert U-238 Atomic Energy Lab kit was taken off shelves two years after making its debut. Now a collector's item, it will cost you around US$6,000—if you can find one!

OUTDOOR FUN

Killer kites: Kite-flying is a competitive sport in countries like India, Pakistan, and Chile. To cut down other kites, kite-flyers use glass- or metal-coated string, which has led to serious injury and death—from slit throats to electrocution. These fatal strings are illegal in Chile and can lead to jail time and a fine. Parts of Pakistan have banned kite-flying altogether, while some states in India have banned the dangerous string.

No-build site: The days of building sandcastles suitable for use as photo backdrops on the beaches of Boracay Island in the Philippines are not only over, but illegal, unless you have a permit. The reason? Builders were tinkering with "the natural terrain of the beach," charging tourists a high fee for photographing their masterworks, and using the picture-perfect sandcastles to distract unsuspecting passersby and then steal from them. Fines are issued for first-timers and people are given jail-time for subsequent offenses.

BY THE NUMBERS: 16. The number of kids, teens, and adults killed in kite-flying related accidents in the state of Gujarat, India, during Uttarayan, the International Kite Festival, in 2018. –*The Times of India*

Snow way: For some reason, it's hard to imagine snow in Saudi Arabia, but snow it does in the northern parts. In 2015, a religious scholar reportedly proclaimed that Islam prohibited the building of snowmen and snow animals, i.e., clear representational models of anything with a soul. Headless or featureless snow sculptures however are okay, as are inanimate objects like, well, castles.

She sells seashells: Pocketing pretty shells and coral as souvenirs may be damaging coastal ecosystems. The Dutch Caribbean island of St. Maarten forbids exporting or importing conch shells and certain types of coral—and if found in your luggage as you arrive or leave, they will be confiscated. In 2019, 200 kg (441 lb.) of conch shells were seized at the airport and returned to the ocean. It's best to look and leave.

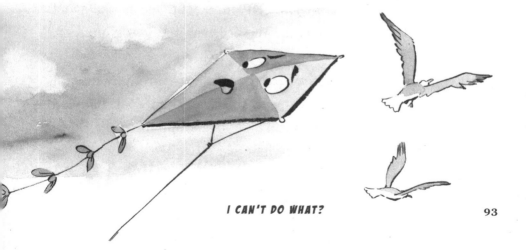

I CAN'T DO WHAT?

Drawing a line in the sand: Jog on it, build with it, bury yourself under it—enjoy your time playing on the beach. Then, when you're done, walk away. Like seashells, taking sand from certain beaches is illegal, and don't even think about selling it. Hawaii can slap you with a fine of up to US$100,000, and in Sardinia, you can be fined up to three thousand euros and risk up to six years in jail.

Food for thought: If your tour-boat guide in Thailand encourages you to toss some food for the fish, don't. It's a crime to feed fish in the ocean and can lead to a fine and up to a year in prison. The reason: to prevent any further damage to the delicate ecosystem, including the coral reefs.

Stop that sled!: Several towns and cities across Canada and the United States have banned tobogganing, also known as sledding, or restricted which hills can host the winter pastime due to reports of accidents—and potential costly lawsuits.

Stay away from the play: Slip 'N Slides are tons of fun—for kids. Back in 1993, the company behind WHAM-O backyard water slides had to release a warning to adults and teens to step away, because the design wasn't suitable for their weight and height. Seven adults and one teenager found out the worst way: with neck injuries or paralysis.

To the point: Playing with metal-tipped lawn darts just doesn't sound prudent. Unfortunately, three American children were killed by such darts when they punctured their skulls, and thousands have sustained injuries. Sales of the game were banned in the United States in 1988 and in Canada a year later.

Up a tree: Climbing a tree is one of those childhood must-dos, but in Toronto, Canada, it's a can't-do if that tree is in a city park. A municipal bylaw having to do with injury and damage states that a person cannot climb any part of a tree (or rock or boulder, for that matter) unless authorized by permit. And those permits are really only issued to those who need them, like an arborist. While tickets are rarely given out, they do happen.

WHAT CAN I DO?: Places around the world are creating laws to save their ecosystems. What environmental protections should your community have?

QUIZ
MATCH THE TOY TO THE REASON IT WAS RECALLED

1. Aqua Dots (2007)
2. Certain hoverboards (2017)
3. Consolidated Stores mini-hammocks (1995)
4. Disney pogo sticks (2011)
5. Hallmark Harry Potter Magic Potion Bottle key chains (2002)
6. LEGO EXPLORE Super Trucks (2006)
7. Magnetix (2006)
8. Nerf N-Strike Recon Blasters (2008)
9. Pokémon balls from Burger King kids meals (1999)
10. Power Wheels Barbie Camper (2019)
11. Sarge die-cast toy car from the movie Cars (2007)
12. Sky Dancers dolls (2000)

A. Could start smoking, catch fire, and/or explode.
B. If child becomes entangled, could lead to strangulation and/or death.
C. Coated with a substance that when swallowed could lead to coma, respiratory depression, and/or seizure.
D. Swallowing detached, loose magnets could lead to intestinal injuries.
E. Could be covered with lead paint.
F. Unpredictable flying could lead to injuries like temporary blindness and mild concussion.
G. Poor quality and/or loose parts could lead to potential falls and lacerations.
H. Could pose suffocation hazard to children under three years old.
I. Could keep running even though the pedal has been released.

HEATHER CAMLOT

J.   Wheels can come off, leaving metal axle exposed and leading to possible puncture injury.
K.   Liquid could leak and lead to problems if ingested.
L.   Skin could get caught, leading to injuries like bruises and welts.

According to the U.S. Consumer Product Safety Commission

CONCLUSION

There's an old saying: "Ignorance of the law is no excuse." It means that even if you don't know something is illegal and you go ahead and do it, you are still responsible and can still be punished. It's up to you to know the laws and rules and to look for signs—like no photographing military bases or no skateboarding on a sidewalk. It doesn't matter whether you agree or not, you have to follow the regulations or face the consequences.

WHAT CAN I DO? If your country holds democratic elections, you may not yet be old enough to vote. But you can remind the adults in your life that to make change, they need to vote, whether mandatory or not, and they shouldn't prevent others from casting their ballot, too.

That said, you should be curious about laws and rules and understand why they came to be. Just because adults agree on something, doesn't mean it's right. If you think a law or rule is unfair, you should try to change it. If you think you're just a kid and can't do anything about it, not so. Laws and rules change all the time: between writing and editing this book, the law against *pretending* to practice witchcraft in Canada disappeared from official government books, and so it disappeared from this book; the law about all young men in South Korea joining the military by the time they turn 28 was updated, allowing Jin, the oldest member of BTS, to postpone military duty.

So, just how can you change rules or laws, or advocate for new ones? Use your voice.

Raise awareness: Let others know about the need for change by spreading the word on social media. Create a video for YouTube or TikTok; share your message on Snapchat; make your statement shareable on Facebook; build a website and tag people and organizations who can help. Then watch your message gain momentum. The Anti-Defamation League also suggests reaching an audience of potential supporters by speaking to traditional media—give an interview to a reporter, create a press release, or write an article for the newspaper.

Organize a protest: You've likely seen at least one protest in recent times—people standing up for issues and incidents in society they don't agree with, from police violence against Black civilians, to denying women's rights, to inaction on Indigenous reconciliation. According to the ADL, protests tell governments how their citizens feel about what's happening in society, shine a spotlight on a cause, and demand change. Gather experts and influencers to speak at your protest, then use momentum from your media platforms; circulate posters; create signs; put up flyers; invite the media to get the word out so others passionate about your cause can show up to your protest, whether it be a march, boycott, strike, walkout, or sit-in, and lend their support.

WHAT CAN I DO?: Ready to raise your voice? Get advice from advocacy organizations. Check out the Canadian Civil Liberties Association's "The Advocacy Toolkit" and the Anti-Defamation League's "10 Ways Youth Can Engage in Activism."

HEATHER CAMLOT

Send an email or letter: Writing a letter or email stating what you believe needs changing, and backing up that demand with key points, facts, statistics, stakes, and a solution, has long been used to put pressure on decision-makers to act. A letter written in your own words shows how passionate you are about the issue, and the more letters the decision-maker receives, the more they will be moved to review the demand and potentially make that change. To start a letter-writing or email campaign, it's best to provide supporters with some basic information (or a template to personalize) from which they can compose their letter—and of course the mailing or email address.

Start a petition: Sometimes it's easier to have that letter already written and have people add their names or signatures to show their support for the cause or issue, big or small, from supporting human rights to protecting the environment. You can start your own petition on Change.org, a site that has helped more than 76,000 petitions get their demands met across the globe. Make sure before signing someone else's petition that you understand it thoroughly and that it's an issue you can get behind.

Join student council: Want to make a change at school to better life for you and your fellow students? Student council or a student alliance, like a gay-straight alliance or Black student alliance, is the place to meet like-minded people, make your issues known, promote student rights, and present ideas and solutions to the principal or other school authority.

Talk to your government representative: The way a law is passed is different from one country to the next, but in a democratic country, citizens just like you can present an idea to your representative, and they can take it to the next step. In the simplest terms, if the representative likes the idea, they can help turn it into

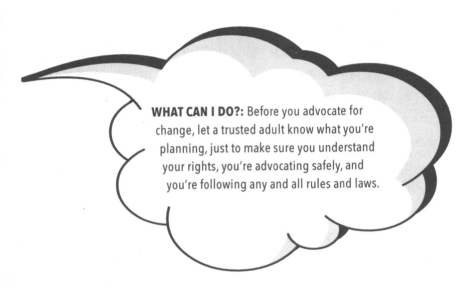

a bill, or a written draft proposal of a law. The bill gets debated in one of the government's legislative houses, and experts are called in for their opinions. A vote is cast, and if the majority of government members says yes, then the bill goes to a second legislative house and the process begins again. If they also vote yes, along with the country's leader or head of state, the bill turns into a law.

What rules and laws do you want to change?

HEATHER CAMLOT

GLOSSARY

AMENDMENT: A formal revision, addition, or improvement to a law or other official document

BAN: To officially forbid something from happening or someone from doing something

BLACKLIST: A list of people or objects to be boycotted, excluded, not trusted, or punished

BYLAW: A law passed by a local government, such as a city or town, and that only applies to that community

CENSOR: To change, cut out, or remove for being unsuitable, objectionable, or offensive

CHALLENGE: An attempt to stop access to certain material, by removing or restricting the objectionable content

CLAUSE: A separate and specific condition included in an agreement or contract

CONTROLLED SUBSTANCE: A drug that is highly restricted by governments to prevent addiction and abuse

DECREE: An official order or decision, usually made by the head of state, with the weight of the law

DEFAMATION: False spoken or written statements that damage a person's reputation. Spoken defamation is called slander. Written defamation, which includes broadcasting like television and radio, is called libel.

EXILE: Living outside one's home country, whether by force or by choice, usually for political reasons

FINE: Money paid as punishment for breaking a rule or a law

LAWS: Formal, legal rules passed by the government that apply equally to a whole society

LEGISLATION: A written law or collection of laws created and approved by government (unlike case law, which is decided by judges)

ORDER: A command, instruction, or direction given by an authoritative figure, such as a leader or judge

ORDINANCE: A law created by a local or municipal government

OUTLAWED: Forbidden or made illegal

POLICY: Official, agreed-upon guidelines or courses of action for certain situations, created by a government, organization, school, business, or person

REGULATION: An official rule created by a government agency with the force of law

RULES: Guidelines on how to act and behave in particular situations

VIOLATION: The act of breaking or infringing on a law, rule, or code of conduct

AUTHOR'S NOTE

The first law class I ever took was an introduction to Canadian law in Grade 11. I loved it. I really can't tell you why, but a great teacher can make that kind of thing happen. I can tell you that I took more law classes throughout my post-secondary education—journalism law, entertainment law, criminology, juvenile delinquency—and still have some of those textbooks. I became fascinated by cases of injustice, like The Dreyfus Affair, Rubin "Hurricane" Carter, and the Chicago 7. I even wrote the Law School Admission Test. As much as I loved reading about crime and legal curiosities, I didn't really want to practice law. Maybe I just wanted to write about it.

The idea for *I Can't Do What?* started out small. I'd tear or print out odd and interesting things I'd read in the newspaper or online and stick them in a folder. Eventually, that folder had a lot of articles about rules and laws I thought were strange. I wrote up a few dozen and shared them with my kids and their friends, who sent back notes with lots of checkmarks and LOLs. I was on to something.

But it was my editor, Peter Carver, who asked the important question: why do these strange laws exist? Suddenly, some of the

HEATHER CAMLOT

rules and laws that I thought were odd had very serious reasons behind them, like China making it illegal for Tibetan monks to reincarnate without permission, or Brazil designating soccer legend Pelé a "national treasure."

Some of the rules and laws in *I Can't Do What?* are funny—like no running the baseball diamond in reverse order and no taking Furbys to the U.S. National Security Agency—but others are angering or frightening. I certainly learned over the course of writing and editing this book to ask a lot of questions, to search out the story behind the story, and to never take anything for granted. While no country may be perfect, I'm grateful to live in Canada, where I can speak up against any law that I believe is strange, harmful, or just plain unfair.

I CAN'T DO WHAT?

ACKNOWLEDGMENTS

A big thank you to my young readers, whose honest feedback inspired me to keep going with this project: Evan Cyr-David, Nicolaas Parsons, Alex Reppin, and Juliana Reppin; to my friends Jennifer Cyr, who makes reading manuscript comments a hilarious event, and Marsha Moshinsky, who eagerly translated Spanish sources for me and offered more background and context to topics she knows well; to my husband, Marc Reppin, who said nothing when confronted with holes in his newspaper from all the articles I cut out, and of course for his unending encouragement; Gitchi Meegwetch/nya:wah-go to Steve Turner for his sensitivity read of Indigenous content; to Montreal lawyer Richard Clare and Halifax lawyer Timothy Matthews for kindly reviewing the manuscript with a professional eye; to Richard Dionne for grasping the value of this project from just a few sample blurbs; to editor Bev Brenna, who came in midway through with passion blazing; to Red Deer Press for its continued support; and to the inimitable Peter Carver, whose editorial eye, humour, and cheer are like no other.

HEATHER CAMLOT

ENDNOTES

P. 46: "Hair must be combed neatly ... and hair pins." Agnes Wayman in "Hints Along General Lines," *Spalding's Athletic Library*, September 1908.

Wayman, Agnes. "Hints Along General Lines." *Spalding's Athletic Library: Official Women's Basket Ball Guide*, no. 318, Sept. 1908, pp. 59–69. Group VII, https://archive.org/details/basketballguidew11amer/page/n1/mode/2up.

P. 55: "Everyone has ... regardless of frontiers." The United Nations General Assembly in the Universal Declaration of Human Rights, 1948.

"Illustrated Version of the Universal Declaration of Human Rights." *United Nations*, United Nations, www.un.org/en/udhrbook/index.shtml#1.

SELECTED SOURCES

I consulted hundreds of sources to research and write this book. Here are some that can help you understand more about laws, rules, and how to advocate for change:

"10 Ways Youth Can Engage in Activism." Anti-Defamation League, www.adl.org/education/resources/tools-and-strategies/10-ways-youth-can-engage-in-activism#.Vg-rqflViko. "The Advocacy Toolkit." *Canadian Civil Liberties Association*, 24 Sept. 2019, ccla.org/29725-2/.

"Resources." *Freedom to Read*, 25 Mar. 2021, www.freedomtoread. ca/resources/.

"Convention on the Rights of the Child." *UNICEF Canada*, https://www.unicef.ca/en/policy-advocacy-for-children/about-the-convention-on-the-rights-of-the-child.

"How Does a Bill Become Law?" *YouTube*, Parliament of Canada,
16 Apr. 2019, www.youtube.com/watch?v=4O8syj77g0Q.

"How Laws Are Made." *Kids in the House*, Office of the Clerk,
U.S. Capitol, kids-clerk.house.gov/grade-school/lesson.
html?intID=17.

"Illustrated Version of the Universal Declaration of Human Rights."
United Nations, United Nations, www.un.org/en/udhrbook/
index.shtml#1.

Paul, Caroline. *You are Mighty: A Guide to Changing the World.*
Bloomsbury Children's Books, New York: 2018.

"What Is the Law?" *What Is the Law – About Canada's System of
Justice*, Department of Justice, Government of Canada,
16 Oct. 2017, www.justice.gc.ca/eng/csj-sjc/just/02.html.

These are just some of the local and international news outlets and
magazines I read to find strange rules and laws. You can start your
own collection, too:

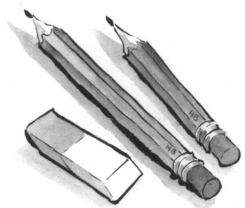

BBC.com
CBC.ca
NPR.org
NYTimes.com
Smithsonianmag.com
Theglobeandmail.com
Theguardian.com